LIVES OF THE SAINTS
Volume I

The Early Church

Written by Bart Tesoriero
Illustrations by Michael Adams

TABLE OF CONTENTS

Library of Congress Control Number: 2012905938
ISBN 1-936020-99-7

SAINT MICHAEL THE ARCHANGEL

Feast Day: September 29

Patron of Police Officers and Emergency Personnel

Saint Michael the Archangel is God's most trusted angel, a heavenly messenger who carries out His every command. Michael means *one who is like God*. Saint Michael is a fierce and powerful warrior, protector, and guardian.

Saint Michael is the guardian of Israel and the protector of the Church. When the angel Lucifer—Satan—and his other bad angels started a war in heaven, Michael and his good angels fought them and drove them out of heaven.

Because he is the protector and defender of God's people as well as the angel who brings souls to judgment, Saint Michael the Archangel is recognized today as the patron of police officers and those who keep others safe.

Prayer to Saint Michael for Police Officers

Saint Michael the Archangel, please bless all who work as police officers and guards. Grant them good judgment in keeping the peace, courage in enforcing the law, and honor in giving justice to all. Amen.

Saint Michael the Archangel, pray for us!

SAINT GABRIEL THE ARCHANGEL

Feast Day: September 29

Patron of Communications/Postal Workers

Gabriel means *God is my strength*. The Archangel Gabriel was always a messenger of important news. He appeared to the prophet Daniel in the Old Testament. Many years later, he appeared to Zechariah, the husband of Elizabeth and father of John the Baptist. Most importantly, Gabriel announced to Mary that God had chosen her to be the mother of His son, Jesus!

The Archangel Gabriel was very good at sharing God's message with people. He helped them to believe in the good things God wanted to do for them and for the whole world. Gabriel is the patron of postal workers and people who work delivering messages to others. Saint Gabriel will help you understand God's message to you as well!

Prayer to Saint Gabriel for Communication Workers

Dear Saint Gabriel, please bless all who deliver messages via TV, radio, the Internet, or the postal service. Help them bring good news to others. Open our hearts also to hear Our Lord speak to us, and to follow Him. Amen.

Saint Gabriel the Archangel, pray for us!

SAINT ANNE

Feast Day: July 26

Patron of Homemakers

Saint Anne was the mother of the Virgin Mary and the grandmother of Jesus. According to tradition, she and her husband, Saint Joachim, had prayed a long time to have a child. God answered their prayer and Anne gave birth to a beautiful little girl whom they named Mary.

Saints Joachim and Anne raised Mary to be a good girl. Saint Anne taught her to cook, to clean, to tend a garden, and most of all, to love God and serve Him.

Today, Saint Anne is remembered as the patron saint of homemakers because she was chosen by God to teach Mary how to be a good mother. Saint Anne and Saint Joachim, the grandparents of Jesus, share the same feast day.

Prayer to Saint Anne for Homemakers

Dear Saint Anne, help all our parents who try to make a happy and comfortable home for us. Please ask God to bless in a special way our mothers and grandmothers. Help all parents everywhere to make a home for Jesus in the hearts of their children. Amen.

Saint Anne, pray for us.

SAINT JOSEPH

Feast Day: March 19

Patron of Fathers, Carpenters, and Homesellers

Saint Joseph was a young carpenter from the town of Nazareth. He was engaged to Mary. Before he and Mary lived together, the Angel Gabriel appeared to Mary and told her that God had chosen her to be the mother of His son. An angel also told Joseph, "Do not be afraid to take Mary as your wife. You are to name her child Jesus." Joseph awoke and did all the angel had told him to do.

After Jesus was born in Bethlehem, an angel spoke to Joseph in a dream, "Get up, take the child and his mother, and flee to Egypt! Stay there until I tell you." Joseph arose quickly and took Jesus and Mary to Egypt. Later they returned to Nazareth, where Joseph worked hard to take care of Mary and Jesus, whom he loved.

Prayer to Saint Joseph for Fathers and Workers

Dear Saint Joseph, you trusted in God and obeyed His commands. Help all fathers to love their families. Help all carpenters to build good homes. Please help homesellers to find good homes for people. O Saint Joseph, I love you! Thank you for being my friend and helper forever. Amen.

Saint Joseph, pray for us.

THE BLESSED VIRGIN MARY

Feast Day: September 8

Patron of Mothers

The Virgin Mary is the most lovely and loving of all God's creations. Through God's grace, Mary was conceived in her mother's womb without Original Sin. Mary in turn gave her whole self and life to God.

God sent the angel Gabriel to Mary when she was a young woman. Gabriel asked her if she would be willing to become the Mother of Jesus. Mary said, "Yes! Let it be done unto me according to thy word." Joseph took Mary as his wife, and Jesus was born.

Mary cared for Jesus and Joseph with all the love in her heart. She was with Jesus when He was born in the stable and when He died on the cross for our sins. Before He died, Jesus gave us Mary to be our Mother as well.

Prayer to Mother Mary for Mothers

Dear Mother Mary, You are the Mother of Jesus and you are my heavenly mother also. Please bless my mom and all mothers, and help them to feel God's love and joy. Amen.

Dear Mother Mary, pray for us.

SAINT MARTHA

Feast Day: July 29
Patron of Cooks and Servers

Saint Martha lived in the town of Bethany with her sister Mary and her brother Lazarus. Jesus loved them and He liked to visit at their home with His apostles. Martha loved to cook and care for Jesus. Mary liked to sit at Jesus' feet and listen to Him speak. One day Martha was upset because Mary did not help her to cook and serve the food for Jesus and His friends. Jesus said to her, "Martha, Martha, you are worried about many things. Only one thing is necessary. Listen to Me."

Martha learned her lesson. Later on, when Lazarus died, Martha trusted Jesus to raise him from the dead. She is recognized today as the patroness of all who cook, clean, and serve others with love.

Prayer to Saint Martha for Cooks and Servers

Dear Saint Martha, you received Jesus in your home and served Him at your table. Help all who serve others to do so with love, joy, and a cheerful heart. Help all of us to remember that in serving others, we are serving Our Lord. Amen.

Saint Martha, pray for us.

SAINT PETER THE APOSTLE

Feast Day: June 29

Patron of Fishermen

Saint Peter was from a town called Bethsaida near the Sea of Galilee. He and his brother Andrew were fishermen when they met Jesus. One day, Jesus told them, "Follow Me, and I will make you fishers of men." The two brothers left their boat and their father and followed Jesus.

Jesus said, "You are Peter, and on this rock I will build My Church." He then gave Peter the keys to the kingdom of heaven. Peter was our first Pope. After Jesus went back to heaven, Peter guided the Church as Jesus had told him.

Peter went to Rome to bring the Gospel to the whole world and to build up the Church. He wrote two Letters, known as Epistles. Saint Peter was crucified upside down by the Emperor Nero and buried on Vatican Hill.

Prayer to Saint Peter for Fishermen

Saint Peter, you left your nets upon the shore and followed Jesus. Please help all fishermen to do well and help all of us to lead others to Jesus by our words and actions. Amen.

Saint Peter, pray for us.

SAINT PAUL

Feast Day: June 29

Patron of Writers

Saint Paul was born as Saul of Tarsus to Jewish parents. He did not believe in Jesus and persecuted the Christians. He held the robes of those who stoned Saint Stephen, the first martyr in the early days of the Church. A martyr is someone who dies as a witness to their faith in Jesus.

One day, a brilliant light flashed around Saul. He fell to the ground and heard the voice of Jesus saying, "Saul, Saul, why are you persecuting Me?" Saul repented of his sins, was baptized, and changed his name to Paul.

Saint Paul preached the Gospel everywhere he went. He suffered much for Christ. Saint Paul was put into prison in Rome, where he was beheaded as a martyr.

Prayer to Saint Paul for Writers

Dear Saint Paul, you wrote many Letters to help your fellow Christians understand and follow Our Lord. Please bless all writers with the grace to inspire others with the words of truth and the fire of love. Amen.

Saint Paul, pray for us.

SAINT MATTHEW, APOSTLE

Feast Day: September 21

Patron of Bankers and Accountants

Saint Matthew was a tax collector. One day Jesus walked by and said, "Follow Me." Matthew left his table and taxes to follow the Messiah. Jesus then came to his house for a feast and was criticized by the Pharisees for eating with tax collectors and sinners. Jesus rebuked the Pharisees. He said, "I came not to call the just, but sinners."

Saint Matthew wrote the first Gospel to teach people about Jesus. He preached the new Faith far and wide, and was martyred. Thus he did follow Jesus, all the way to death and eternal life in heaven.

Because of his work with money as a tax collector, Saint Matthew is recognized today as the patron of bankers.

Prayer to Saint Matthew for Bankers

Dear Saint Matthew, you left everything to follow Jesus when He called you. Please help all bankers and accountants to be honest and trustworthy. Help them to follow Jesus, whatever the cost. Amen.

Saint Matthew, pray for us.

SAINT VERONICA

Feast Day: July 12

Patroness of Photographers

According to tradition, Saint Veronica is the woman who wiped the face of Jesus with her veil as He carried the cross on His way to Calvary. The cloth was imprinted with the image of Jesus' face. The relic is still preserved in Saint Peter's Basilica, and the memory of Veronica's act of charity is commemorated in the Stations of the Cross.

It is unclear what happened to Saint Veronica after the Crucifixion. Some say she brought the image to Rome and miraculously healed the Emperor Tiberius of an ailment.

Because of the image that appeared on her veil, Saint Veronica is recognized today as the patron of photographers.

Prayer to Saint Veronica for Photographers

Dear Saint Veronica, you looked with pity on Jesus in His suffering. You offered Him your veil to wipe His face. In return for your great kindness, He left upon that cloth the imprint of His holy face. Help all photographers to see the face of Jesus in everyone they meet. Amen.

Saint Veronica, pray for us.

SAINT LUKE THE EVANGELIST

Feast Day: October 18

Patron of Doctors

Saint Luke the Evangelist was born in Antioch, Syria. His parents were Greek. He was a doctor who traveled with Saint Paul on his missionary journeys. Saint Luke ministered with Saint Paul, and helped to heal people who were sick in their bodies and in their souls. In his Epistle to the Colossians, Saint Paul refers to Saint Luke as "the beloved doctor."

Saint Luke wrote the third Gospel as well as the exciting Acts of the Apostles, giving us a history of the infant Church. Historians also think that Saint Luke may have painted some of the earliest icons of Our Lady, including the famous Black Madonna in Poland.

Saint Luke was Saint Paul's faithful companion, and after Paul's death, Luke also died as a martyr in Greece.

Prayer to Saint Luke for Doctors

Dear Saint Luke, you helped to heal many people in body and soul. Help all doctors to do their work carefully and well. Dear God, please help doctors to always treat their patients with compassion and skill. In Jesus' name we pray. Amen.

Saint Luke, pray for us.

SAINT JOHN THE APOSTLE

Feast Day: December 27

Patron of Booksellers

Jesus called John at a very young age to follow Him and become an Apostle. Saint John stood faithfully with Mary by Jesus as He hung on the Cross. Jesus in turn gave His Mother to John, who took her into his home. During the era of the new Church, Saint John preached in Jerusalem and Ephesus. He later wrote a Gospel and three Epistles.

The emperor tried to kill John in boiling oil, but God delivered him. Saint John wrote the Book of Revelation and died in the year 100. Saint John is recognized today as the patron of book sellers, art dealers and printers.

Prayer to Saint John for Booksellers

Dear Saint John, you loved Jesus so much in your life that you are called the beloved apostle. Jesus entrusted His Mother to you as your Mother. Through your words and works, you have taught us how to love God. Bless all who work in printing and publishing, and help them to also draw people to God as they serve Him through their work. Amen.

Saint John the Apostle, pray for us!

SAINT CECILIA

Feast Day: November 22

Patroness of Musicians and Singers

Cecilia, a beautiful and noble Roman maiden, had given herself as a virgin to God. Her parents, however, gave her in marriage to Valerian, a pagan. On their wedding night, Cecilia told her husband that an angel defended her. If he wished to see the angel, he must first be baptized. Valerian heard heavenly music, was baptized and he gave himself to God. His brother also accepted Jesus as His Savior.

The Roman ruler killed Valerian and his brother because they were Christians. Then he commanded Cecilia to be burned in a furnace. But the flames had no power over her, and so the executioner beheaded her. In the year 177, the virgin Saint Cecilia gave back her pure spirit to Christ. Today she is the patron saint of musicians.

Prayer to Saint Cecilia for Musicians

Saint Cecilia, you honored Jesus on earth and you will sing God's praises forever in heaven. Help those who sing or play music to honor God also with their hands and voices. May they compose beautiful music to help other people enjoy and honor God as well. Amen.

Saint Cecilia, pray for us.

SAINT CHRISTOPHER

Feast Day: July 25

Patron of Travelers and Truck Drivers

Saint Christopher was a very strong man who lived long ago. He carried travelers on his back across a nearby river. One cold stormy night, a little Child knocked on the door of Christopher's cottage and asked him for a ride across the river. As they crossed the water, the Child grew heavier and heavier until Christopher thought they would both be swept away by the rushing stream. "Who are you?" he asked.

The Child answered, "I am Jesus, and I bear the world on my shoulders." Christopher knelt in worship and received his name, which means *Christ-Bearer*. After that night, he preached about Christ to all who came his way, and he died as a martyr for the Child. Saint Christopher is the patron of all travelers and truck drivers.

Prayer to Saint Christopher for Truck Drivers

Mighty Saint Christopher, you carried Jesus on your shoulders. Jesus carries us all on His shoulders. Please pray with us to God that He will help all truck drivers and travelers to be safe and alert. May they see Christ and serve Him in the people they meet along their way. Amen.

Saint Christopher, pray for us.

SAINT LUCY

Feast Day: December 13

Patron of Those with Eye Ailments

Saint Lucy was born to a rich family in Sicily around the year 283. Lucy gave herself to Jesus as His special bride at an early age. Not knowing this, her mother promised Lucy in marriage to a young pagan man named Paschasius. Paschasius told the governor that Lucy was a Christian. The governor ordered his guards to take out her eyes. God miraculously restored Lucy's eyesight, and the governor ordered his guards to set a fire around her. Again, God saved her. Finally, the guards killed Lucy with a dagger.

In Sicily and Italy, there is a story that Saint Lucy travels door to door in a donkey-drawn wagon with gifts for children on her feast day. That is why she is also the patron of salespeople.

Prayer to Saint Lucy for Those with Eye Ailments

Dear Saint Lucy, you brightened the lives of those around you by sharing good things with others. Please pray for all who suffer with eye ailments and blindness. Through your prayers, may God give them perfect vision. May they use their eyes for His greater honor and glory. Amen.

Saint Lucy, pray for us.

THE EARLY CHURCH

Jesus told His first apostles, "Follow Me!" He had come from God the Father, and He alone knew the way back to God. Jesus taught His followers how to become friends with God. Jesus died and arose from the dead to take away the sins of the world and to send out His Holy Spirit. He gave His disciples the power to become the children of God, their heavenly Father who loved them so very much.

Before He ascended into heaven after His death and Resurrection, Jesus commanded His apostles to preach the Gospel. On the feast of Pentecost, Mother Mary and the followers of Jesus were filled with the Holy Spirit. They began to tell everyone the Good News, that they too could become friends with God because of what Jesus had done. The first people who believed and were baptized are known as the Early Church, the first Catholic Christians.

Many of these first followers of Jesus suffered and died as martyrs, or witnesses, for their faith in Jesus. Because God was with them, they were not afraid. They are the first heroes and heroines of our faith.

Dear Saints of the Early Church, thank you for believing in Jesus even when others did not understand. Please help me to be not afraid to love God and to serve Him. Amen.